FUMED OAK

An Unpleasant Comedy in
Two Scenes

by
NOEL COWARD

PLAYED IN "TO-NIGHT AT 8.30"

SAMUEL FRENCH

LONDON
NEW YORK SYDNEY TORONTO HOLLYWOOD

© 1935 BY NOEL COWARD
COPYRIGHT (ACTING EDITION) 1938 BY NOEL COWARD

Rights of Performance by Amateurs are controlled by Samuel French Ltd, 52 Fitzroy Street, London W1P 6JR, and they, or their authorized agents, issue licences to amateurs on payment of a fee. **It is an infringement of the Copyright to give any performance or public reading of the play before the fee has been paid and the licence issued.**

The Royalty Fee indicated below is subject to contract and subject to variation at the sole discretion of Samuel French Ltd.

> Basic fee for each and every
> performance by amateurs   Code E
> in the British Isles

The publication of this play does not imply that it is necessarily available for performance by amateurs or professionals, either in the British Isles or Overseas. Amateurs and professionals considering a production are strongly advised in their own interests to apply to the appropriate agents for consent before starting rehearsals or booking a theatre or hall.

ISBN 0 573 02079 5

Please see page iv for further copyright information

FUMED OAK

First produced at the Opera House, Manchester, and subsequently at the Phœnix Theatre, Charing Cross Road, London, W.C.2, in January, 1936, with the following cast of characters:

HENRY GOW	*Noel Coward.*
DORIS (*His Wife*)	*Gertrude Lawrence.*
ELSIE (*His Daughter*) . . .	*Moya Nugent.*
MRS. ROCKETT (*His Mother-in-law*) .	*Alison Leggatt.*

SCENE 1.—Morning.
SCENE 2.—Evening.

The action of the play passes in the sitting-room of the Gows' house in South London.

The time is the present day.

COPYRIGHT INFORMATION
(See also page ii)

This play is fully protected under the Copyright Laws of the British Commonwealth of Nations, the United States of America and all countries of the Berne and Universal Copyright Conventions.

All rights, including Stage, Motion Picture, Radio, Television, Public Reading, and Translation into Foreign Languages, are strictly reserved.

No part of this publication may lawfully be reproduced in ANY form or by any means — photocopying, typescript, recording (including video-recording), manuscript, electronic, mechanical, or otherwise — or be transmitted or stored in a retrieval system, without prior permission.

Rights of Performance by Amateurs are controlled by Samuel French Ltd, 52 Fitzroy Street, London W1P 6JR, and they, or their authorized agents, issue licences to amateurs on payment of a fee. **It is an infringement of the Copyright to give any performance or public reading of the play before the fee has been paid and the licence issued.**

Licences are issued subject to the understanding that it shall be made clear in all advertising matter that the audience will witness an amateur performance; that the names of the authors of the plays shall be included on all announcements and on all programmes; and that the integrity of the authors' work will be preserved.

The Royalty Fee is subject to contract and subject to variation at the sole discretion of Samuel French Ltd.

In Theatres or Halls seating Four Hundred or more the fee will be subject to negotiation.

In Territories Overseas the fee quoted in this Acting Edition may not apply. A fee will be quoted on application to our local authorized agent, or if there is no such agent, on application to Samuel French Ltd, London.

VIDEO RECORDING OF AMATEUR PRODUCTIONS

Please note that the copyright laws governing video-recording are extremely complex and that it should not be assumed that any play may be video-recorded for *whatever purpose* without first obtaining the permission of the appropriate agents. The fact that a play is published by Samuel French Ltd does not indicate that video rights are available or that Samuel French Ltd controls such rights.

FUMED OAK
SCENE I

The Gows' sitting-room is indistinguishable from several thousand other suburban sitting-rooms. The dominant note is refinement. There are French windows at the back opening on to a narrow lane of garden. These are veiled discreetly by lace curtains set off by pieces of rather faded blue casement cloth. There is a tiled fireplace on the L.; an upright piano between it and the window; a fumed-oak sideboard on the R. and, below it, a door leading to the hall, the stairs and the front door. There is a fumed-oak dining-room set consisting of a table and six chairs; a sofa; an armchair in front of the fire; and a plentiful sprinkling over the entire room of ornaments and framed photographs.

When the CURTAIN *rises it is about eight-thirty on a spring morning. Rain is trickling down the windows and breakfast is laid on the table.*

MRS. ROCKETT *is seated in the armchair by the fire; on a small table next to her is a workbasket. She is a fattish, grey-looking woman dressed in a blouse and skirt and a pepper-and-salt jumper of artificial silk. Her pince-nez snap in and out of a little clip on her bosom and her feet are bad, which necessitates the wearing of large quilted slippers in the house.* DORIS, *aged about thirty-five, is seated* R. *of the table reading a newspaper propped up against the cruet. She is thin and anæmic, and whatever traces of past prettiness she might have are obscured by the pursed-up, rather sour gentility of her expression. She wears a nondescript coat-frock, a slave bangle and a necklace of amber glass beads.* ELSIE, *her daughter, aged about fourteen, is sitting opposite to her, cutting her toast into strips in order to dip them into her boiled egg. She is a straight-haired ordinary-looking girl dressed in a navy blue school dress with a glacé red leather waist-belt.*

There is complete silence broken only by the occasional rattle of a spoon in a cup or a sniffle from ELSIE, *who has a slight head cold.*

HENRY GOW *comes into the room. He is tall and spare, neatly dressed in a blue serge suit. He wears rimless glasses and his hair is going grey at the sides and thin on the top. He sits down at the table, up stage, without a word.* DORIS *automatically rises and goes out, returning in a moment with a plate of haddock, which she places in front of him and resumes her place.* HENRY *pours himself out some tea.* DORIS, *without looking at him, being re-immersed in the paper, passes him the milk and sugar.* HENRY *stretches for toast across the table.*

The silence continues until ELSIE *breaks it.*

ELSIE. Mum?

DORIS. What?

ELSIE. When can I put my hair up?

DORIS (*snappily*). When you're old enough.

ELSIE. Gladys Pierce is the same age as me and she's got hers up.

DORIS. Never you mind about Gladys Pierce, get on with your breakfast.

ELSIE. I don't see why I can't have it cut. That would be better than nothing.

(*This remark is ignored.*)

Maisie Blake had hers cut last week and it looks lovely.

DORIS. Never you mind about Maisie Blake neither. She's common.

ELSIE. Miss Pritchard doesn't think so. Miss Pritchard likes Maisie Blake a lot, she said it looked ever so nice.

DORIS (*irritably*). What?

ELSIE. Her hair.

DORIS. Get on with your breakfast. You'll be late.

ELSIE (*petulantly*). Oh, Mum——

DORIS. And stop sniffling. Sniffle, sniffle, sniffle! Haven't you got a handkerchief?

ELSIE. Yes, but it's a clean one.

DORIS. Never mind, use it.

MRS. ROCKETT. The child can't help having a cold.

DORIS. She can blow her nose, can't she, even if she has got a cold?

ELSIE (*conversationally*). Dodie Watson's got a terrible cold, she's had it for weeks. It went to her chest and then it went back to her head again.

MRS. ROCKETT. That's the worst of schools, you're always catching something.

ELSIE. Miss Pritchard's awful mean to Dodie Watson, she said she'd had enough of it.

DORIS. Enough of what?

ELSIE. Her cold.

(*There is silence again, which is presently shattered by the wailing of a baby in the house next door.*)

MRS. ROCKETT. There's that child again. It kept me awake all night.

DORIS. I'm very sorry, I'm sure. (*She picks up the newspaper.*)

MRS. ROCKETT (*fiddling in her work basket*). I wasn't blaming you.

DORIS. The night before last it was the hot-water pipes.

MRS. ROCKETT. You ought to have them seen to.

DORIS. You know as well as I do you can't stop them making that noise every now and then.

MRS. ROCKETT (*threading a needle*). I'm sure I don't know why you don't get a plumber in.

DORIS (*grandly*). Because I do not consider it necessary.

MRS. ROCKETT. You would if you slept in my room—gurgle gurgle gurgle all night long—it's all very fine for you, you're at the end of the passage.

Doris (*with meaning*). You don't have to sleep there.

Mrs. Rockett. What do you mean by that?

Doris. You know perfectly well what I mean.

Mrs. Rockett (*with spirit*). Listen to me, Doris Gow. I've got a perfect right to complain if I want to, and well you know it. It isn't as if I was staying here for nothing.

Doris. I really don't know what's the matter with you lately, Mother, you do nothing but grumble.

Mrs. Rockett. Me, grumble! I like that, I'm sure. That's rich, that is.

Doris. Well, you do. It gives me a headache.

Mrs. Rockett. You ought to do something about those headaches of yours. They seem to pop on and off at the least thing.

Doris. And I wish you wouldn't keep passing remarks about not staying here for nothing.

Mrs. Rockett. Well, it's true, I don't.

Doris. Anyone would think we was taking advantage of you, to hear you talk.

Mrs. Rockett. Well, they wouldn't be far wrong.

Doris. Mother, how can you! You're not paying a penny more than you can afford.

Mrs. Rockett. I never said I was. It isn't the money, it's the lack of consideration.

(Elsie *puts her exercise book away in her satchel.*)

Doris. Pity you don't go and live with Nora for a change.

Mrs. Rockett. Nora hasn't got a spare room.

Doris. Phyllis has, a lovely one, looking out over the railway. I'm sure her hot-water pipes wouldn't keep you awake, there isn't enough hot water in them.

Mrs. Rockett. Of course, if I'm not wanted here, I can always go to a boarding-house or a private hotel.

Doris. Catch you!

Mrs. Rockett. I'm not the sort to outstay my welcome anywhere . . .

Doris. Oh, for heaven's sake don't start that again . . . (*She bangs the paper down on the table.*)

Mrs. Rockett (*addressing the air*). It seems as though some of us had got out of bed the wrong side this morning.

Elsie. Mum, can I have some more toast?

Doris. No.

Elsie. I could make it myself over the kitchen fire.

Doris. No, I tell you. Can't you understand plain English? You've had quite enough and you'll be late for school.

Mrs. Rockett. Never mind, Elsie, here's twopence. (*Taking it out of her purse.*) You can buy yourself a sponge-cake at Barrets.

Elsie (*rising and taking the twopence*). Thanks, Grandma.

Doris. You'll do no such thing, Elsie. I'm not going to have a child of mine stuffing herself with cake in the middle of the High Street.

Mrs. Rockett (*sweetly*). Eat it in the shop, dear.

Doris. Go on, you'll be late.

Elsie. Oh, Mum, it's only ten to.

Doris. Do as I tell you.

Elsie. Oh, all right.

(*She crosses in front of the table and goes sullenly out of the room and can be heard scampering noisily up the stairs.*)

Mrs. Rockett (*irritatingly*). Poor little soul.

Doris. I'll trouble you not to spoil Elsie, Mother.

Mrs. Rockett. Spoil her! I like that. Better than half-starving her.

Doris (*hotly*). Are you insinuating...

Mrs. Rockett. I'm not insinuating anything. Elsie's getting a big girl, she only had one bit of toast for her breakfast and she used that for her egg. I saw her.

Doris (*rising and putting away the paper in the sideboard drawer*). It's none of your business, and in future I'd be much obliged if you'd keep your twopences to yourself. (*She returns to her seat at the table.*)

(Henry *rises and fetches the paper out.*)

Mrs. Rockett (*hurt*). Very well, of course if I'm to be abused every time I try to bring a little happiness into the child's life . . .

Doris. Anyone would think I ill-treated her the way you talk.

Mrs. Rockett. You certainly nag her enough.

Doris. I don't do any such thing—and I wish you'd leave me to bring up my own child in my own way.

Mrs. Rockett. That cold's been hanging over her for weeks and a fat lot you care——

Doris (*rising and getting tray from beside the sideboard*). I've dosed her for it, haven't I ? The whole house stinks of Vapex. What more can I do ?

Mrs. Rockett. She ought to have had Doctor Bristow last Saturday when it was so bad. He'd have cleared it up in no time.

Doris (*putting tray on her chair and beginning to clear things on to it*). You and your Doctor Bristow.

Mrs. Rockett. Nice thing if it turned to bronchitis.

(Doris *throws scraps into the fire.*)

Mrs. Henderson's Muriel got bronchitis, all through neglecting a cold; the poor child couldn't breathe, they had to have two kettles going night and day——

Doris. I suppose your precious Doctor Bristow told you that.

Mrs. Rockett. Yes, he did, and what's more, he saved the girl's life, you ask Mrs. Henderson.

Doris. Catch me ask Mrs. Henderson anything, stuck up thing. . . .

Mrs. Rockett. Mrs. Henderson's a very nice ladylike woman, just because she's quiet and a bit reserved you say she's stuck up . . .

Doris. Who does she think she is, anyway, Lady Mountbatten ? (*She takes the cruet to the sideboard.*)

Mrs. Rockett. Really, Doris, you make me tired sometimes, you do really.

Doris. If you're so fond of Mrs. Henderson it's a pity you don't see more of her. I notice you don't go there often.

Mrs. Rockett (*with dignity*). I go when I am invited.

Doris (*triumphantly*). Exactly.

Mrs. Rockett. She's not the kind of woman that likes people popping in and out all the time. We can't all be Amy Fawcetts.

Doris. What's the matter with Amy Fawcett? (*She takes the teapot to the sideboard.*)

Mrs. Rockett. Well, she's common for one thing, she dyes her hair for another, and she's a bit too free and easy all round for my taste.

Doris. She doesn't put on airs, anyway.

Mrs. Rockett. I should think not, after the sort of life she's led.

Doris (*takes bread to sideboard*). How do you know what sort of a life she's led?

Mrs. Rockett. Everybody knows, you only have to look at her; I'm a woman of the world, I am, you can't pull the wool over my eyes——

(Elsie *comes into the room wearing a mackintosh and a tam-o'-shanter.*)

Elsie. Mum, we want a new roll of toilet paper.

Doris. How many times have I told you ladies don't talk about such things!

Elsie (*as she stamps over to the piano and begins to search untidily through a pile of music on it*). It's right down to the bit of cardboard.

Doris (*scraping the bottom of her cup on the saucer*). Don't untidy everything like that, what are you looking for?

Elsie. "The Pixies' Parade," I had it last night.

Doris. If it's the one with the blue cover it's at the bottom.

Elsie. It isn't—oh dear, Miss Pritchard will be mad at me if I can't find it.

Mrs. Rockett (*rising*). Perhaps you put it in your satchel, dear. Here, let me look—— (*She opens* Elsie's *satchel which is hanging over the back of a chair and fumbles in it.*) Is this it?

Elsie. Oh yes, thanks, Grandma.

Doris. Go along now, for heaven's sake, you'll be late.

(Mrs. Rockett *helps* Elsie *on with her satchel.*)

Elsie. Oh, all right, Mum. Good-bye, Grandma, good-bye, Dad.

Henry. Good-bye.

Mrs. Rockett. Good-bye, dear, give Grandma a kiss.

(Elsie *does so.*)

Doris (*pushing* Elsie *out of the door*). Don't dawdle on the way home.

Elsie. Oh, all right, Mum.

(*She goes out. The slam of the front door shakes the house.*)

Doris (*irritably*). There now.

Mrs. Rockett (*with studied politeness*). If you are going down to the shops this morning, would it be troubling you too much to get me a reel of white cotton? (*She sits in the armchair.*)

Doris (*tidying the piano*). I thought you were coming with me.

Mrs. Rockett. I really don't feel up to it.

Doris. I'll put it on my list.

(*She takes a piece of paper out of the sideboard drawer and scribbles on it.*)

Mrs. Rockett. If it's out of your way, please don't trouble. It'll do another time.

Doris. Henry, it's past nine.

Henry (*without looking up*). I know.

Doris. You'll be late.

Henry. Never mind.

Doris. That's a nice way to talk, I must say.

Mrs. Rockett. I'm sure if my Robert had ever lazed about like that in the mornings, I'd have thought the world had come to an end.

Doris. Henry'll do it once too often, mark my words. (*She crosses behind* Henry.)

Mrs. Rockett (*biting off her thread*). Well, that corner's finished. (*She puts away her embroidery and starts to knit.*)

Doris (*to* Henry). You'll have to move now, I've got to clear. (*Taking first his saucer, then his cup, from his hand.*)

(Henry *rises absently.*)

Mrs. Rockett. Where's Ethel?
Doris. Doing the bedroom.

(Henry *quietly goes out of the room.*)

(*Throwing more scraps on the fire.*) Look at that wicked waste.
Mrs. Rockett. What's the matter with him?
Doris. Don't ask me, I'm sure I couldn't tell you.
Mrs. Rockett. He came in very late last night, I heard him go into the bathroom.

(*There is a pause.*)

That cistern makes a terrible noise.
Doris (*emptying crumbs from cloth into fire and folding it*). Does it indeed!
Mrs. Rockett. Yes, it does.
Doris (*slamming the teapot on to the tray*). Very sorry, I'm sure.
Mrs. Rockett. Where'd he been?
Doris. How do I know?
Mrs. Rockett. Didn't you ask him?
Doris. I wouldn't demean myself.
Mrs. Rockett. Been drinking?
Doris. No.
Mrs. Rockett. Sounded very like it to me, all that banging about.
Doris. You know Henry never touches a drop.
Mrs. Rockett. I know he says he doesn't.
Doris. Oh, do shut up, Mother, we're not all like Father. (*She puts the cloth in the sideboard drawer, then scrapes grease with her nail from the green cloth on the table.*)
Mrs. Rockett. You watch your tongue, Doris Gow, don't let me hear you saying anything against the memory of your poor father.

Doris. I wasn't.

Mrs. Rockett (*belligerently*). Oh yes, you were, you were insinuating again.

Doris (*hoisting up the tray*). Father drank and you know it, everybody knew it. (*She moves* L.)

Mrs. Rockett. You're a wicked woman.

Doris. It's true.

Mrs. Rockett. Your father was a gentleman, which is more than your husband will ever be, with all his night-classes and his book reading—night-classes, indeed!

Doris (*poking the fire*). Who's insinuating now?

Mrs. Rockett (*angrily*). I am, and I'm not afraid to say so.

Doris. What of it?

Mrs. Rockett (*with heavy sarcasm*). I suppose he was at a night-class last night?

Doris (*loudly*). Mind your own business.

(Henry *comes in, wearing his mackintosh and a bowler hat.*)

Henry. What's up?

Doris. Where were you last night?

Henry. Why?

Doris. Mother wants to know and so do I.

Henry. I was kept late at the shop and I had a bit of dinner in town.

Doris. Who with?

Henry. Charlie Henderson.

(*He picks up the paper off the table and goes out. The baby next door bursts into fresh wails.*)

Mrs. Rockett. There goes that child again. It's my belief it's hungry.

Doris. Wonder you don't go and give it twopence to buy sponge-cake.

(*She pulls the door open with her foot and goes out with the tray as the lights fade on the scene.*)

SCENE II

It is about seven-thirty in the evening. ELSIE *is sitting at the piano practising with the loud pedal firmly down all the time.* MRS. ROCKETT *is sitting in her chair by the fire, but she is dressed in her street things and wearing a black hat with a veil.* DORIS, *also in street clothes, is trying on paper patterns.*

There is a cloth across the upstage end of the table on which is set a loaf, a plate of cold ham, a saucer with two tomatoes in it, a bottle of A1 sauce and a teapot, tea-cup, sugar basin and milk jug.

HENRY *comes in, taking off his mackintosh. He gives one look round the room and goes out into the hall again to hang up his things.* ELSIE *stops playing and comes over to* DORIS.

ELSIE. Mum, can we go now?
DORIS. In a minute.
ELSIE. We'll miss the Mickey.
DORIS. Put on your hat and don't worry.
ELSIE (*grabbing her hat from the sideboard*). Oh, all right.

(HENRY *re-enters.*)

DORIS. Your supper's all ready, the kettle's on the gas stove when you want it. (*Folding up paper patterns.*) We've had ours.
HENRY. Oh!
DORIS. And you needn't look injured, either.
HENRY. Very well. (*He crosses in front of the table.*)
DORIS. If you managed to get home a bit earlier it'd save a lot of trouble all round.
HENRY (*amiably*). Sorry, dear. (*He warms his hands at the fire.*)
DORIS. It's all very fine to be sorry, you've been getting later and later these last few weeks, they can't keep you overtime every night.

Henry. All right, dear, I'll tell them.

Doris. Here, Elsie, put these away in the cupboard. Mind your fingers with the scissors.

(*She hands her a pile of material and pieces of paper.* Elsie *obediently takes them and puts them in the left-hand cupboard of the sideboard.*)

Henry (*sitting at the table*). Cold ham, what a surprise!

Doris (*looking at him sharply*). What's the matter with it? (*She puts on her coat.*)

Henry. I don't know, yet.

Doris. It's perfectly fresh, if that's what you mean.

(Elsie *crosses to* L.C.)

Henry. Why are you all so dressed up?

Elsie. We're going to the pictures. (*She picks up her bag and gloves.*)

Henry. Oh, I see.

Doris (*putting on her gloves*). You can put everything on the tray when you've finished and leave it in the kitchen for Ethel.

Henry. Good old Ethel.

Doris (*surprised*). What?

Henry. I said good old Ethel.

Doris. Well, it sounded very silly, I'm sure.

Mrs. Rockett (*scrutinizing him*). What's the matter with you?

Henry. Nothing, why?

Mrs. Rockett. You look funny.

Henry. I feel funny.

Mrs. Rockett. Have you been drinking?

Henry. Yes.

Doris. Henry!

Mrs. Rockett. I knew it!

Henry. I had a whisky and soda in town and another one at the Plough.

Doris (*astounded*). What for?

Henry. Because I felt like it.

Doris. You ought to be ashamed of yourself.

HENRY. I'm going to have another one too, a bit later on.

DORIS. You'll do no such thing.

HENRY. That hat looks awful.

DORIS (*furiously*). Don't you speak to me like that.

HENRY. Why not?

DORIS (*slightly non-plussed*). Because I won't have it—that's why not.

HENRY. It's a common little hat and it looks awful.

DORIS (*with an admirable effort at control*). Now listen to me, Henry Gow, the next time I catch you drinking and coming home here and insulting me, I'll . . .

HENRY (*interrupting her gently*). What will you do, Dorrie?

DORIS (*hotly*). I'll give you a piece of my mind, that's what I'll do.

HENRY (*rising*). It'll have to be a very little piece. You can't afford much! (*He laughs delightedly at his own joke.*)

DORIS. I'd be very much obliged if you'd kindly tell me what this means?

HENRY. I'm celebrating.

DORIS. Celebrating! What do you mean, celebrating?

HENRY (*up* L.C.). To-night's our anniversary.

DORIS (R.C.). Don't talk so soft, our anniversary's not until November.

HENRY. I don't mean that one. To-night's the anniversary of the first time I had an affair with you and you got in the family way.

DORIS (*shrieking*). Henry! (*She moves down stage.*)

HENRY (*delighted with his carefully calculated effect*). Hurray!

DORIS (*beside herself*). How dare you say such a dreadful thing, in front of the child, too.

HENRY (*in romantic tones*). Three years and a bit after that wonderful night our child was born! (*Lapsing into his normal voice.*) Considering all the time you took forming yourself, Else, I'm surprised you're not a nicer little girl than you are.

Doris. Go upstairs, Elsie.
Henry. Stay here, Elsie.

(Elsie *dithers.*)

Doris. Do as I tell you.
Elsie (l.c.). But, Mum . . .
Doris. Mother, take her for God's sake! There's going to be a row.

(Mrs. Rockett *rises.*)

Henry (*firmly*). Leave her alone and sit down. Leave her alone and sit down.

(Mrs. Rockett *hesitates.* Elsie *sits on the piano stool.*)

Mrs. Rockett (*subsiding into the chair*). Well, I never, I . . .
Henry (*happily*). See? It works like a charm.
Doris. A fine exhibition you're making of yourself, I must say.
Henry. Not bad, is it? As a matter of fact, I'm rather pleased with it myself.
Doris. Go to bed!
Henry. Stop ordering me about, see. (*Crossing* c.) What right have you got to nag at me and boss me? No right at all. I'm the one that pays the rent and works for you and keeps you. What do you give me in return, I'd like to know? Nothing. (*He bangs the table.*) I sit through breakfast while you and Mother wrangle. You're too busy being snappy and bad-tempered even to say good-morning. I come home tired after working all day and ten to one there isn't even a hot dinner for me; here, see this ham? That's what I think of the ham. (*He throws it at her feet.*) And the tomatoes and the A.1 bloody sauce! (*He throws them too.*)
Doris (*screaming*). Henry! All over the carpet. (*Getting plate and knife.*)
Henry (*throwing the butter-dish face downwards on the floor*). And that's what I think of the carpet. (*He moves* l.)

Doris (*scraping up the butter on to the plate*). That I should live to see this! That I should live to see the man I married make such a beast of himself!

Henry. Stop working yourself up into a state, you'll need all your control when you've heard what I'm going to say to you.

Doris (*making a move to him*). Look here . . .

Henry. Sit down. And you. And you.

(Mrs. Rockett *and* Elsie *sit again.*)

I'm afraid you'll have to miss the pictures for once.

Doris. Elsie, you come with me.

Mrs. Rockett. Yes, go on, Ducks.

(Doris *makes a movement towards the door, but* Henry *is too quick for her. He locks the door and slips the key into his pocket.*)

Henry. I've been waiting for this moment for fifteen years, and believe me it's not going to be spoilt for me by you running away.

Doris (*on the verge of tears*). Let me out of this room.

Henry. You'll stay where you are until I've had my say.

Doris. Let me out of this room. Don't you lay your hands on me. (*Bursting into tears and sinking down at the table.*) Oh! Oh! Oh! . . .

(*She falls into the chair* R. *of the table as he pushes her.*)

Elsie (*starting to cry too*). Mum—— Oh, Mum . . .

Henry. Here you, shut up, go and get the port out of the sideboard and give some to your mother . . . Go on, do as I tell you.

(Elsie, *terrified and hypnotized into submission, goes to the sideboard cupboard and brings out a bottle of invalid port and some glasses, snivelling as she does so.* Doris *continues to sob.*)

That's right. (*He crosses up* C.)

Mrs. Rockett (*quietly*). You drunken brute, you!

HENRY (*cheerfully*). Worse than that, Mother, far worse. Just you wait and see.

(ELSIE *sits on the chair* L. *of the table.*)

MRS. ROCKETT (*ignoring him*). Take some port, Dorrie, it'll do you good.

DORIS. I couldn't touch any—it'd choke me . . .

HENRY (*pouring some out*). Come on—here . . .

DORIS. Keep away from me.

HENRY. Drink it and stop snivelling.

DORIS. I'll never forgive you for this, never, never, never, as long as I live. (*She gulps down some port.*)

HENRY (*noting her gesture*). That's better.

MRS. ROCKETT. Pay no attention, Dorrie, he's drunk.

HENRY. I'm not drunk. I've only had two whiskies and sodas, just to give me enough guts to take the first plunge. You'd never believe how scared I was, thinking it over in cold blood. I'm not scared any more though, it's much easier than I thought it was going to be. My only regret is that I didn't come to the boil a long time ago, and tell you to your face, Dorrie, what I think of you, what I've been thinking of you for years, and this horrid little kid, and that old bitch of a mother of yours.

MRS. ROCKETT (*shrilly*). Henry Gow!

HENRY. You heard me, old bitch was what I said and old bitch was what I meant.

MRS. ROCKETT. Let me out of this room. (*Rising and crossing to the window.*) I'm not going to stay here and be insulted—I'm not . . .

(*They all rise.*)

HENRY. You're going to stay here just as long as I want you to.

MRS. ROCKETT. Oh, am I? We'll see about that. . . .

(*With astonishing quickness she darts over to the window and manages to drag one open.* HENRY *grabs her by the arm.*)

HENRY. No, you don't.

MRS. ROCKETT. Let go of me.

DORIS. Oh, Mother, don't let the neighbours know all your business.

HENRY. Not on your life!

MRS. ROCKETT (*suddenly screaming powerfully*). Help! Help! Police! Help! Mrs. Harrison—help! . . .

(HENRY *drags her away from the window, turns her round and gives her a light slap on the face; she staggers against the piano. Meanwhile he shuts the window again, locks it and pockets the key.*)

DORIS (*looking at him in horror—runs to below the table*). Oh, God! Oh, my God!

ELSIE (*bursting into tears again*). Oh, Mum, Mum, he hit Grandma! Oh, Mum . . .

(*She runs to* DORIS, *who puts her arm round her protectively.*)

MRS. ROCKETT (*gasping*). Oh—my heart! I think I'm going to faint—— Oh—my heart—— Oh—— Oh—— Oh, dear——

(MRS. ROCKETT *slides on to the floor, perceptibly breaking her fall by clinging on to the piano stool.*)

DORIS. Mother!

HENRY. Stay where you are.

(HENRY *goes to the sideboard and pours out a glass of water.* DORIS, *disobeying him, runs over to her mother.* ELSIE *wails.*)

Stand out of the way, Doris, we don't all want to get wet.

(*He approaches with the glass of water.* MRS. ROCKETT *sits up weakly.*)

MRS. ROCKETT (*in a far-away voice*). Where am I?

HENRY. Number Seventeen Cranworth Road, Clapham.

Mrs. Rockett. Oh—oh, dear!

Henry. Look here, Mother, I don't want there to be any misunderstanding about this. I liked slapping you just now, see? It was lovely, and if you don't behave yourself and keep quiet I shall slap you again. Go and sit in your chair and remember if you feel faint the water's all ready for you.

(*He helps her up and escorts her to her chair by the fire. She collapses into it and looks at him balefully.*)

Now then. Sit down, Dorrie, you look silly standing about.

Doris (*with a great effort at control—sits in* Henry's *chair*). Henry——

Henry (*slowly, but very firmly*). Sit down! And keep her quiet or I'll fetch her one too.

Doris (*with dignity*). Come here, Elsie.

(Elsie *sits on the chair* R. *of the table.*)

(*Banging her back.*) Shut up, will you

Henry. That's right.

(*He walks round the room slowly and in silence, looking at them with an expression of the greatest satisfaction on his face. Finally he goes over to the fireplace;* Mrs. Rockett *jumps slightly as he approaches her, but he smiles at her reassuringly. Meanwhile* Doris, *recovering from her fear, is beginning to simmer with rage; she remains still, however, watching.*)

(*Sitting on the piano stool.*) Now then. I'm going to start, quite quietly, explaining a few things to you.

Doris. Enjoying yourself, aren't you?

(Mrs. Rockett *wipes her neck with her handkerchief.*)

Henry. You've said it.

Doris (*gaining courage*). You'll grin on the other side of your face before I've done with you.

Henry (*politely*). Very likely, Dorrie, very likely indeed!

Doris. And don't you Dorrie me either! Coming home here drunk, hitting poor Mother and frightening Elsie out of her wits.

Henry. Out of her what?—— Do her good, do 'em both good, a little excitement in the home. God knows, it's dull enough as a rule.

Doris (*with biting sarcasm*). Very clever, oh, very clever, I'm sure.

Henry. Sixteen years ago to-night, Dorrie, you and me had a little rough and tumble in your Aunt Daisy's house in Stansfield Road, do you remember?

Doris. Henry—— (*Pointing to* Elsie.)

Henry (*ignoring her*). We had the house to ourselves, it being a Sunday, your aunt had popped over to the Golden Calf with Mr. Simmonds, the lodger, which, as the writers say, was her wont——

Mrs. Rockett (*rising*). This is disgusting, I won't listen to another word.

Henry (*rising—rounding on her*). You will! Shut up!

(Mrs. Rockett *sits*.)

Doris. Pay no attention, Mother, he's gone mad.

Henry. Let me see now, where was I? Oh yes, Stansfield Road. You'd been after me for a long while, Dorrie. I didn't know it then, but I realized it soon after. You had to have a husband, what with Nora married and Phyllis engaged, both of them younger than you, you had to have a husband, and quick, so you fixed on me. You were pretty enough and I fell for it hook, line and sinker; then, a couple of months later you told me you'd clicked, you cried a hell of a lot, I remember, said the disgrace would kill your mother if she ever found out. I didn't know then that it'd take a sight more than that to kill that leathery old mare——

Mrs. Rockett (*bursting into tears*). I won't stand it, I won't! I won't!

Henry (*rising above her sobs*). I expect you were in on the whole business, in a refined way of course, you knew what was going on all right, you knew that Dorrie was no more in the family way than I was, but we got married; you both saw to that, and I chucked up all the plans I had for getting on, perhaps being a steward in a ship and seeing a bit of the world. Oh yes, all that had to go and we settled down in rooms and I went into Ferguson's Hosiery.

DORIS. I've given you the best years of my life and don't you forget it.

HENRY. You've never given me the best of anything, not even yourself. You didn't even have Elsie willingly.

DORIS (*wildly*). It's not true—stop up your ears, Elsie, don't listen to him, he's wicked—he's wicked——

(ELSIE *makes to do it.*)

HENRY (*grimly*). It's true all right, and you know it as well as I do.

DORIS (*shrilly*). It was only right that you married me. It was only fair! You took advantage of me, didn't you? You took away my innocence. It was only right that you paid for it.

HENRY. Come off it, Dorrie, don't talk so silly. I was the innocent one, not you. I found out you'd cheated me a long long time ago, and when I found out, realized it for certain, I started cheating you. (*He leans on the chair* L. *of the table.*) Prepare yourself, Dorrie, my girl, you're going to be really upset this time. I've been saving! Every week for over ten years I've been earning a little bit more than you thought I was. I've managed, by hook and by crook, to put by five hundred and seventy-two pounds—d'you hear me?—five hundred and seventy-two pounds!

MRS. ROCKETT (*jumping to her feet*). Henry! You never have—it's not true——

DORIS (*also jumping up*). You couldn't have—you'd have given it away—I should have found out——

HENRY. I thought that'd rouse you, but don't get excited.

(MRS. ROCKETT *sits again.*)

I haven't got it on me, it's in the bank. And it's not for you, it's for me—all but fifty pounds of it, that much is for you, just fifty pounds, the last you'll ever get from me——

DORIS. Henry! You couldn't be so cruel! You couldn't be so mean!

HENRY. I've done what I think's fair and what I think's fair is a damn sight more than you deserve. To start with I've transferred the freehold of this house into your name so you'll always have a roof over your head—you can take in lodgers at a pinch, though God help the poor bleeders if you do!

DORIS. Five hundred and seventy-two pounds! You've got all that and you're going to leave me to starve! (*She takes off her coat and puts it on the chair down* R.)

HENRY. Cut out the drama, Dorrie, and have a look at your mother's savings bank book—I bet you'll find she's got enough to keep you in comfort till the day you die. She soaked her old man plenty, I'm sure—before he took to soaking himself!

MRS. ROCKETT. It's a lie! (*She rises.*)

HENRY. Now listen to me! Mother Machree—you've 'ad one sock in the jaw this evening and you're not just asking for another, you're sitting up and begging for it.

(DORIS *pulls the curtains back.*)

MRS. ROCKETT. I'll have you up for assault. I'll have the police on you, my fine fellow!

HENRY. They'll have to be pretty nippy—my boat sails first thing in the morning.

DORIS (*horrified*). Boat! (*At the window.*)

(MRS. ROCKETT *sits.*)

HENRY (*moving up* C.). I'm going away. I've got my ticket here in my pocket, and my passport. My passport photo's a fair scream, I wish I could show it to you, but I don't want you to see the nice new name I've got.

DORIS (*crossing to him*). Henry, you can't do it, I can have you stopped by law. It's desertion.

HENRY. That's right, Dorrie, you've said it. Desertion's just exactly what it is.

DORIS (*breathlessly*). Where are you going, you've got to tell me. Where are you going?

HENRY. Wouldn't you like to know? Maybe Africa, maybe China, maybe Australia. There are lots of places in the world you know nothing about, Dorrie. You've often laughed at me for reading books, but I've found out a hell of a lot from books.

(DORIS *sits on* HENRY'S *chair*.)

There are islands in the South Seas, for instance, with coco palms and turtles and sunshine all the year round—you can live there for practically nothing, then there's Australia or New Zealand; with a little bit of capital I might start in a small way sheep farming. Think of it; miles and miles of open country stretching as far as the eye can see—good food and fresh air—that might be very nice, that might suit me beautifully. Then there's South America. There are coffee plantations there, and sugar plantations, and banana plantations. If I go to South America I'll send you a whole crate. 'Ave a banana, Dorrie! 'Ave a banana!

DORIS. Henry, listen to me, you can't do this dreadful thing, you can't! If you don't love me any more, think of Elsie.

HENRY (*still in his dream*). Then there's the sea, not the sea we know at Worthing with the tide going in and out regular and the band playing on the pier. The real sea's what I mean. The sea that Joseph Conrad wrote about, and Rudyard Kipling and lots of other people, too, a sea with whacking great waves and water spouts and typhoons and flying-fish and phosphorus making the foam look as if it was lit up.

(DORIS *turns up stage on her chair*.)

Those people knew a thing or two, I can tell you. They knew what life could be like if you give it a chance. They knew there was a bit more to it than refinement and fumed oak and getting old and miserable with nothing to show for it. I'm a middle-aged man, but my health's not too bad, taken all round. There's still time for me to see a little bit of real life before I conk out. I'm still fit enough to do a job of work—real work, mind you—not bowing and scraping and wearing myself out showing fussy old cows the way to the lace and the china ware and the bargain basement. (*He crosses to the fireplace.*)

DORIS (*hysterically*). God will punish you, you just see if He doesn't, you just see——

HENRY. God's been punishing me for fifteen years, it's high time He laid off me now. He's been punishing me good and proud for being damn fool enough to let you get your claws into me in the first place——

DORIS (*changing her tactics*). Henry, have pity, for God's sake have pity.

HENRY. And don't start weeping and wailing either, because it won't wash. I know you, Dorrie, I know you through and through. You're frightened now, scared out of your wits, but give you half a chance and you'd be worse than ever you were. You're a bad lot, Dorrie, not what the world would call a bad lot but what I call a bad lot. Mean and cold and respectable.

DORIS (*rising and going to him*). Listen to me, Henry, you've got to listen—you must. You can't leave us to starve, you can't throw us on to the streets—if I've been a bad wife to you, I'm sorry—I'll try to be better, really I will, I swear to God I will—— You can't do this. If you won't forgive me, think of Elsie, think of poor little Elsie——

HENRY. Poor little Elsie, my eye! I think Elsie's awful, I always have ever since she was little. She's never done anything but whine and snivel and try to get something for nothing——

ELSIE (*wailing*). Oh, Mum, did you hear what he said? Oh, Dad, oh dear——

MRS. ROCKETT (*crossing and comforting her*). There, there, dear, don't listen to him—— (*She sits in the chair* L. *of the table.*)

HENRY. Elsie can go to work in a year or so; in the

meantime, Dorrie, you can go to work yourself, you're quite a young woman still and strong as an ox.—Here's your fifty pounds——

(*He takes an envelope out of his pocket and throws it on to the table. Then he goes towards the door.* DORIS *rushes after him and hangs on to his arm.*)

DORIS. Henry, Henry, you shan't go, you shan't——

(ELSIE *rises.*)

HENRY (*struggling with her*). Leave hold of me. (*He goes to the door.*)

DORIS (*following him*). Mother, Mother—help—help me, don't let him go——

MRS. ROCKETT. Run, Doris, run!

(HENRY *frees himself from her and, taking her by the shoulders, forces her back into a chair, then he unlocks the door and opens it.*)

(ELSIE *sits in the* O. *chair.*)

HENRY. I'm taking my last look at you, Dorrie. I shall never see you again as long as I live—— It's a dream come true.

(DORIS *buries her head in her arms and starts to sob loudly.* MRS. ROCKETT *sits transfixed, staring at him murderously.*)

(*Quietly.*) Three generations. Grandmother, Mother and Kid. Made of the same bones and sinews and muscles and glands, millions of you, millions just like you. You're past it now, Mother, you're past the thick of the fray, you're nothing but a music-hall joke, a mother-in-law with a bit of money put by. Dorrie, the next few years will show whether you've got guts or not. Maybe what I'm doing to you will save your immortal soul in the long run. That'd be a bit of all right, wouldn't it? I doubt it, though, your immortal soul's too measly. You're a natural bully and a cheat and I'm sick of the sight of you; I should also like to take this opportunity of saying that I hate that bloody awful slave bangle and I always have. As for you, Elsie, you've got a chance, it's a slim one, I grant you, but still it's a chance. If you learn to work and be independent and, when the time comes, give what you have to give freely and without demanding lifelong payment for it, there's just a bit of hope that you'll turn into a decent human being. At all events, if you'll take one parting piece of advice from your cruel, ungrateful father, you'll spend the first money you ever earn on having your adenoids out. Good-bye, one and all. Nice to have known you!

(*The wails of* DORIS *and* ELSIE *rise in volume as he goes jauntily out, slamming the door behind him.*)

CURTAIN.

PROPERTY PLOT

As used at the Phœnix Theatre

1. *Square Oak Table* with green table-cloth, white table-cloth, 3 knives and forks, 3 cups and saucers, spoons, (tea in 2 cups), teapot with tea, 1 plate with cooked haddock, 1 plate with egg-cup and egg-shell and small piece of toast and spoon, 1 plate with cut brown loaf. Large cruet (c.), jug of milk, small white jug. Sugar basin, glass dish of marmalade and spoon. Toast-rack and 1 piece of toast, *Daily Mirror*. (*Note*.—crockery used willow pattern.) Exercise book and pencil. Butter in butter dish.
2. *Oak Sideboard* with fern, 2 blue vases, glass biscuit barrel, glass jug of water and tumbler. 2 pink and yellow china bowls.

    In cupboard: bottle half-filled port, 2 wine-glasses.
    In drawer: material, paper pattern, scissors.
2A. Black tray below sideboard.
3. Maple tub settee.
4. Upright piano with vase of Pampas grass and music.
5. Maroon leather armchair.
6. Small round bamboo table with work-basket, embroidery, knitting, purse with coppers, scissors, thimble, handkerchief.
7, 8, 9. Oak chairs (on chair L. of table, satchel with piece of music).
10. Oak armchair.
11. Round piano stool.
12. Music-rack with music.
13. Oak curb.
14. Oak fireplace (practical) and mantelpiece, small clock, large vase with paper spills, 4 small vases.
15. Steel fire-irons on stand.
16. Square coal scuttle.

Old Axminster carpet down.
Lace curtains to windows.
2 small brackets with aspidistra and geraniums.
Practical blue curtains on oak rod.
Oak mirror over sideboard.
Picture over settee.
Picture over piano.
Small picture (seascape) down stage L.
Grass matting outside window.

Off Stage R.
 Coat stand and hanging rack.
 Plate of ham.
 Door slam.
In Change.
 Set on table : material, paper pattern, scissors, tablecloth on top half of table with plate of ham, knife and fork, cup, saucer, spoon, plate with 2 tomatoes, bottle of A1 sauce, plate with two slices brown bread, plate with butter.
Personal Property (HENRY).
 Envelope with £50 in bank-notes (not opened).